Guest

Name

Thoughts

Guests

Name	Thoughts

Guests

Name

Thoughts

Guests

Name

Thoughts

Guests

Name

Thoughts

Guests

Name | Thoughts

Guests

Name

Thoughts

Guests

Name | Thoughts

Guests

Name

Thoughts

Guests

Name | Thoughts

Guests

Name	Thoughts

Guests

Name	Thoughts

Guests

Name

Thoughts

Guests

Name

Thoughts

Guests

Name | Thoughts

Guests

Name	Thoughts

Guests

Name

Thoughts

Guests

Name

Thoughts

Guests

Name

Thoughts

Guests

Name	Thoughts

Guests

Name	Thoughts

Guests

Name

Thoughts

Guests

Name	Thoughts

Guests

Name	Thoughts

Guests

Name

Thoughts

Guests

Name	Thoughts

Guests

Name

Thoughts

Guests

Name	Thoughts

Guests

Name	Thoughts

Guests

Name	Thoughts

Guests

Name | Thoughts

Name	Thoughts

Guests

Name

Thoughts

Guests

Name

Thoughts

Guests

Name

Thoughts

Guests

Name

Thoughts

Guests

Name	Thoughts

Guests

Name	Thoughts

Guests

Name	Thoughts

Guests

Name | Thoughts

Name	Thoughts

Guests

Name | Thoughts

Guests

Name	Thoughts

Guests

Name

Thoughts

Guests

Name

Thoughts

Guests

Name

Thoughts

Guests

Name Thoughts

Guests

Name

Thoughts

Guests

Name

Thoughts

Guests

Name | Thoughts

Guests

Name	Thoughts

Guests

Name | Thoughts

Guests

Name

Thoughts

Guests

Name	Thoughts

Guests

Name

Thoughts

Guests

Name	Thoughts

Guests

Name

Thoughts

Guests

Name	Thoughts

Guests

Name

Thoughts

Guests

Name | Thoughts

Guests

Name

Thoughts

Guests

Name

Thoughts

Guests

Name

Thoughts

Guests

Name	Thoughts

Guests

Name

Thoughts

Guests

Name

Thoughts

Guests

Name

Thoughts

Guests

Name | Thoughts

Guests

Name

Thoughts

Guests

Name	Thoughts

Guests

Name

Thoughts

Guests

Name	Thoughts

Guests

Name	Thoughts

Guests

Name

Thoughts

Guests

Name

Thoughts

Guests

Name	Thoughts

Guests

Name

Thoughts

Guests

Name	Thoughts

Guests

Name

Thoughts

Guests

Name	Thoughts

Guests

Name

Thoughts

Guests

Name	Thoughts

Guests

Name	Thoughts

Guests

Name	Thoughts

Guests

Name

Thoughts

Guests

Name

Thoughts

Guests

Name

Thoughts

Guests

Name

Thoughts

Guests

Name	Thoughts

Guests

Name

Thoughts

Guests

Name	Thoughts

Guests

Name

Thoughts

Guests

Name

Thoughts

Guests

Name

Thoughts

Guests

Name

Thoughts

Guests

Name

Thoughts

Guests

Name

Thoughts

Guests

Name

Thoughts

Guests

Name

Thoughts

Guests

Name	Thoughts

Guests

Name

Thoughts

Guests

Name

Thoughts

Guests

Name

Thoughts

Guests

Name | Thoughts

Guests

Name

Thoughts

Guests

Name	Thoughts

Guests

Name	Thoughts

Guests

Name	Thoughts

Guests

Name

Thoughts

Guests

Name

Thoughts

Guests

Name

Thoughts

Guests

Name

Thoughts

Guests

Name

Thoughts

Guests

Name

Thoughts

Guests

Name

Thoughts

Guests

Name | Thoughts

Guests

Name

Thoughts

Guests

Name

Thoughts

Guests

Name	Thoughts

Guests

Name	Thoughts

Guests

Name

Thoughts

Guests

Name	Thoughts

Guests

Name	Thoughts

Guests

Name

Thoughts

Guests

Name

Thoughts

Guests

Name

Thoughts

Guests

Name	Thoughts

Guests

Name | Thoughts

Guests

Name

Thoughts

Guests

Name

Thoughts

Guests

Name

Thoughts

Guests

Name

Thoughts

Guests

Name	Thoughts

Guests

Name	Thoughts

Guests

Name

Thoughts

Guests

Name

Thoughts

Guests

Name

Thoughts

Guests

Name | Thoughts

Guests

Name

Thoughts

Guests

Name Thoughts

Guests

Name	Thoughts

Guests

Name

Thoughts

Guests

Name

Thoughts

Guests

Name

Thoughts

Guests

Name

Thoughts

Guests

Name

Thoughts

Guests

Name

Thoughts

Guests

Name

Thoughts

Guests

Name

Thoughts

Guests

Name

Thoughts

Guests

Name

Thoughts

Guests

Name

Thoughts

53234419R00085

Made in the USA
Lexington, KY
26 June 2016